OUR NAMES
Are MANY

The Black Woman's Book of Days
edited by Terri Jewell

THE CROSSING PRESS
FREEDOM, CALIFORNIA

For information on bulk purchases or group discounts for this and other Crossing Press titles, please contact our Special Sales Manager at 800-777-1048.

ISBN 0-89594-801-X

Photo by René Dawson

Terri L. Jewell was born in Louisville, Kentucky, in 1954. She was a poet, feminist, scholar, and human rights activist. Her works reflect a strong commitment to Afrocentricity as well as feminism. Her writings appeared in hundreds of journals, including *The African American Review, Women of Power, The American Voice, Sinister Wisdom, Calyx,* and *The Black Scholar.* She is the author of *The Succulent Heretic,* a chapbook of poems, and the editor of *The Black Woman's Gumbo Ya-Ya: Quotations by Black Women.* She died in 1995. Her spirit lives on in her friends and in this book.

Dear Elaine,

I thought that if I'm going to put in a plea for *Our Names Are Many; The Black Woman's Book of Days*, it had best be now.

My initial vision for this project was to be able to present to Black women something special, something not found anywhere else. Having herstorical facts for each day of the week was only part of it.

The other part was to have visuals—even if just a few—that were unique, depicting Black women more as *people* than as celebrities or "ideals." The "ideal" Black woman, generally, is not "too dark," not "too African-looking," not "too fat," not "too nappy-headed"…We Black women find scant material that acknowledges us as *who we are*.

I like your idea of including some photographs of famous Black women already available as postcards at The Crossing Press. And I had to smile when you mentioned you simply *had* to have a photograph of Sojourner Truth. It reminded me of when John Gill insisted that I have a quote by Coretta Scott King for *The Black Woman's Gumbo Ya-Ya*. I realized that Coretta Scott King was an important point of reference for John. And so he got his quote!

You mentioned that you were not interested in including photographs of unknown Black women. I have received some black-and-white photographs from the Smithsonian Institution Photographic Archives. They are exquisite, Elaine. They are priceless images that we Black women do not see and would love to see more of! I have shown them to some of my friends here, and they gasp when they see them. It does not matter that they are "unknown." They are "unknown" only in that the viewer does not know their names.

However, that does not matter at all. The photographs show Black women who lived and have now passed—Black women who look like the Black women in our own lives! These photographs are Black women posed in gowns and flowered hats and *attitude*. These are women we Black women recognize and know so very well because they truly belong to us!

"Recognizable" Black women are fine. But we get those images *constantly*—Alice Walker, Zora Neale Hurston, Mahalia Jackson, Audre Lorde, and so many others who are highly visible. But the majority of us are not *visible* at all, even when we are standing in front of someone's eyes. Having yet *another* publication with the same women's photographs in it will not sell the book to Black women! We seek something always different just as other women do.

So that is my plea. Sojourner Truth is played out among us Black women. I do realize that she is a point of reference for *white* women, but we have so many other "sheroes." I have made it my business to point them out. And if it makes any difference, one of the unknown women looks very much like Sojourner! (Smile) Imagine if *only* a handful of "renowned" white women were forever thrown out as deserving recognition! It would work your last nerve after ten or fifteen years, wouldn't it! Well, that is what we Black women are facing. And I bet there are plenty of visuals of "unknown" white women printed. But that is never an issue.

So that is my plea. *Please* give it some thought. I do realize that your concern is whether or not the book sells to the broadest audience. That is your bottom line. My job is to work hard to meet that challenge and to give something to Black women that they cannot find anywhere else. We *both* can be nourished in this.

Sincerely,
Terri

Terri Jewell did not have time to finish the work on this calendar before she died. Her friend Stephanie Byrd completed the work. The Crossing Press is indebted to her.

FOREWORD

by Stephanie Byrd

In bringing to life this perpetual calendar, Terri had in mind the African griots of the past, sitting and articulating the history of their cultures, event by event and name by name. In this way the history of their people was passed on. This calendar continues this tradition of remembrance, though in written—not verbal—form.

Two key words from the Lucumi language were significant for Terri while she was working on this project: *ebo* and *ache*. Ebo is the bridge that makes it possible for ache, or power, to continue for generations of Lucumi people. For Terri, this calendar is a thing done—an accomplishment of the past—and a bridge to things to do.

Terri worked for a long time on this project. It is a book for you to record reminders to pick up the okra for tonight's gumbo. It is for you to record important dates, final examinations, birthdays, anniversaries, successes, setbacks—the material of living. It can also serve as a reminder of what was accomplished in the past and what can be accomplished today and in the future. It is a registry for your hopes, dreams, and innermost plans. And when it is full, it will serve as a personal history of your life, alongside the lives of those who have gone before you.

JANUARY

1   **Clementine Hunter,** "The Black Grandma Moses," died on this day in 1988 at age 101.

Today is the last day of Kwanzaa: *imani* ("faith").

Queen Makeda of Sheba (now Ethiopia), the great biblical beauty who melted King Solomon's heart in a song, succeeded her father in 1005 B.C. and ruled for 50 years. **2**

3   The first great woman in recorded history and the first Egyptian warrior queen, **Pharaoh Hatsheput**, reigned about 1472–1458 B.C.

Mary Ellen Pleasant, the shrewdest business person—male or female—in San Francisco during the early 1800s gold rush, died during this month in 1904. **4**

Photo by James Van Der Zee, "Children's Dance Class," 1928

"For I am my mother's daughter, and the drums of Africa still beat in my heart. They will not let me rest while there is a single Negro boy or girl without a chance to prove his worth."

—Mary McLeod Bethune (1875–1955)
"Clarifying Our Vision with the Facts"
Journal of Negro History, January 1938

JANUARY

5 The **Candaces,** a line of Ethiopian queens, ruled from 300 B.C. to A.D. 300. They erected magnificent palaces and tombs and ushered in a cultural renaissance.

Leah Chase, a master chef in the Creole tradition, was born this day in 1923. **6**

7 The first Black opera singer to perform with the New York Metropolitan Opera House, **Marian Anderson,** played Ulrica in Verdi's *The Masked Ball* in 1955.

Pauli Murray, the first Black woman Episcopal priest, was ordained at the National Cathedral in Washington, D.C., in 1977. **8**

JANUARY

9 In 1896, **Julia Hammonds** received a patent for a device to hold yarn while knitting.

10 Brooklyn's first Black schoolteacher, **Sarah Lee Brown Fleming,** was born in 1875.

11 The oldest known representational figure of the human body, the **Venus of Willendorf** (15,000–10,000 B.C., found near Vienna, Austria) was carved by Blacks of the Grimaldi people living in Europe. The Grimaldis lived in Europe before Cro-Magnon or Caucasoid peoples.

12 **Queen Cleopatra** was born in 69 B.C. She reigned, with her two brothers and her son, from 51 to 30 B.C.

The women of this world...must exercise leadership quality, dedication, concern and commitment which is not going to be shattered by inanities and ignorance and idiots who would view our cause as one that is violative of the American dream of equal rights for everyone.

—Barbara Jordan, born 1936, address, International Women's Year Conference, Austin, TX, 1975

...I am not a quitter. I will fight until I drop. That is a strength that is in my sinew. It is just a matter of having some faith in the fact that as long as you are able to draw breath in this universe you have a chance.

—Cicely Tyson

"My command stands firm like the mountains, and the sun's disk shines and spreads rays over the titulary of my august person, and my falcon rises above the kingly banner unto all eternity."

—Hatshepsut (1503–1482 B.C.)
quoted in *The Remarkable Women of Ancient Egypt*,
by Barbara Lesko (1978)

JANUARY

13 **Hilda Hutchinson Jefferson** was the first Black woman to serve as mayor *pro tempore* of Charleston, South Carolina. She was appointed in 1975. She served terms in 1976, 1984, and 1992.

Tituba, a slave woman, was accused of being a witch in 1692. She was tried in the colonial courts of Salem, Massachusetts, and sentenced to death, but she confessed and was later released from jail. **14**

15 **Julie Dash**'s *Daughters of the Dust,* the first nationally distributed feature film by a Black woman in the United States, opened this day in 1992 at the Film Forum in New York City.

The first Black woman brigadier general in the air force, **Marcelite Harris,** was born on this day in 1943. **16**

JANUARY

17 In 1961, "Please, Mr. Postman," recorded by the **Marvelettes** female vocal group, gave Motown Records of Detroit its first number 1 hit.

Queen Nefertiti of Egypt reigned in the fourteenth century B.C. **18**

19 **Lucy Terry** is considered to be the first poet of African descent in the Colonies. Her poem "Bar's Fight," about the Deerfield massacre, was written in 1746.

On this day in 1993, **Maya Angelou** became the first Black woman to write and deliver an inaugural poem, "On the Pulse of Morning." *(See also April 4.)* **20**

JANUARY

21 **Fannie M. Jackson Coppin**, one of the first Black women to graduate from an American college (Oberlin, in 1865), died in 1913.

Sculptor **Meta Vaux Warrick Fuller** exhibited at the 101st Annual Exhibition (1906) of the Pennsylvania Academy of Fine Arts in Philadelphia. She received great acclaim abroad when her work was exhibited in Paris in 1903. **22**

We haven't got guns we haven't got nothing we are just going to fight with our talk—that's the only thing. We are not prepared to fly away like chickens.

—Regina Ntongana, South African activist

Photo by Elizabeth Williams

Better to live as a rogue and a bum,
a lover all treat as a joke
to hang out with a crowd of comfortable drunks,
than crouch in a hypocrite's cloak.

—Mahsati (twelfth century)
Selected Quatrains, #1, trans. by Deirdre Lashgari
Women Poets of the World (1983)

JANUARY

23 **Bernice Collins**, born in 1957, became the first Black woman clown with the Ringling Brothers, Barnum and Bailey circus in 1977.

The best known of the few Asante heroines, **Queen Mother Yaa Asantewa of Ejisu**, rallied the Asante against the British in 1900. The ensuing war has been given her name. She died around 1921. **24**

25 In 1966, **Constance Baker Motley** became the first Black woman federal judge.

Carol Moseley-Braun became the first Black woman elected to the U.S. Senate (1992) and the fourth Black to serve in the Senate's history. The first Black licensed aviatrix, **Bessie Coleman**, was born on this day in 1893. **Angela Davis** was born this day. She ran twice for vice-president of the U.S. on the communist party ticket. *(See also May 20.)* **26**

JANUARY

27 Gospel diva **Mahalia Jackson** died on this day in 1972.

Black folklore authority and author, **28** **Zora Neale Hurston**, died on this day in 1960 at age 69.

29 **Oprah Winfrey**, born on this day in 1954, is the first woman to own and produce her own talk show.

West African **Queen Amina of Hausa** **30** reigned in the fifteenth or sixteenth century. She was the Hausa's most famous ruler and greatest warrior and created the only Hausa empire.

From my own study of the
question, the colored woman
deserves greater credit for
what she has done and is
doing than blame for what she
cannot so soon overcome.

—Fannie Barrier Williams

I am deliberate and afraid of
nothing.

—Audre Lorde from "New Year's Day"

There was one of two things I
had a right to, liberty or death.
If I could not have one, I
would have the other, for no
man should take me alive.

—Harriet Ross Tubman

Sojourner Truth, photo courtesy of Burton Historical Collection

"I know that it feels a kind o' hissin' and ticklin' like to see a colored woman get up and tell you about things, and woman's rights. We have all been thrown down so low that nobody thought we'd ever get up again. But we have been long enough trodden now. We will come up again, and now I am here."

—Sojourner Truth (1797–1883)
Speech, the Mob Convention,
Broadway Tabernacle, New York City, September 8, 1853

JANUARY/FEBRUARY

31 **Etta Moten** became the first Black actress to perform at the White House when she sang for President and Mrs. Franklin D. Roosevelt in 1934.

The first stamp in the U. S. Postal Service's Black Heritage series, the **Harriet Tubman** stamp, was issued on this day in 1978. Today is also the first day of **Black History Month.** **1**

2 **Margaret Bailey** was promoted this month in 1970 to become the first Black woman to hold the rank of colonel in the U.S. Army Nurses Corps.

In 1956, **Autherine Lucy** became the first Black student to enroll at the University of Alabama. **3**

FEBRUARY

4 **Rosa Parks**, who ushered in the civil rights movement by her staunch refusal to relinquish her seat to a white and move to the back of the bus, was born this day in 1913. Her act sparked a 381-day bus boycott in Montgomery, Alabama.

Victoria Lillian Cumber published *Sepia Hollywood* magazine from 1941 to 1945. She published this magazine at a time when new publishing ventures were discouraged by paper shortages and other war-related problems. **5**

6 **Ruby Doris Robinson**, a young member of the Student Nonviolent Coordinating Committee (SNCC), initiated the "jail-in" form of protest in 1961 in Rock Hill, South Carolina.

Credited with putting the "swing" in European classical music, child prodigy **Hazel Dorothy Scott** was born in 1920. **7**

FEBRUARY

8 **Alice Walker**, Pulitzer Prize author of *The Color Purple*, was born on this day in 1944.

9 **Juanita Jewel Craft**, a teacher and fundraiser, was elected to a seat on the Dallas City Council at age 73. She was born on this day in 1902.

Too much of our history is consigned to anonymity, which makes it all the more desirable that we humanize our past, whenever possible, by bringing alive the names and faces of those who went before us.

—Sisters in Study from *Charting the Journey*

"It seems less degrading to give one's self, than to submit to compulsion. There is something akin to freedom in having a lover who has no control over you, except that which he gains by kindness and attachment."

—Harriet Brent Jacobs (1818–1896)
Incidents in the Life of a Slave Girl (1861),
1973 reprint edited by Lydia Maria Child

FEBRUARY

10 On this day in 1927, **Leontyne Price**, the great American soprano, was born. Her performance as Leonora in *Il Travatore* received a 42-minute ovation, one of the longest in the history of the Metropolitan Opera.

11 The first female known to petition the African Methodist Episcopal Church for authority to preach, **Jarena Lee**, was born in 1783. Her petition was denied, but she preached anyway as an itinerant preacher.

12 **Jackie Torrence**, one of America's foremost story-tellers, was born on this day in 1944. She has recorded numerous albums and specializes in African American tales, Appalachian mountain lore, and ghost stories.

13 In 1882, **Matilda Sissieretta Jones** appeared with the World's Fair Colored Opera Company at Carnegie Hall in New York City. She sang for the Prince of Wales in 1888 and for President Harrison in 1892.

FEBRUARY

14 **Yvonne Clark**, the first Black woman engineer in Nashville, was also the first woman to major in mechanical engineering at Howard University. She was born in Louisville, Kentucky, in 1925.

15 With the blessing of the established Quaker leadership, **Mother Rebecca Jackson**, born in 1795, formed the only known urban, Black-led Shaker "OutFamily"—meaning outside the existing Quaker communities.

16 **Bessie Smith**, the "Empress of the Blues," made her first recording for Columbia Records on this day in 1923. "Down Hearted Blues," written by **Alberta Hunter** and **Lovie Austin**, became Columbia Records' first popular hit.

17 Internationally recognized historian, educator, lawyer, and human rights activist, **Mary Frances Berry**, was born on this day in 1938.

I, me, I am a free black woman.
My grandmothers and their mother
knew this and kept their silence
to compost up their strength,
kept it hidden
and played the game of deference
and agreement and pliant will.

It must be known now how that silent legacy
nourished and infused such a line
such a close linked chain
to hold us until we could speak
until we could speak out
loud enough to hear ourselves
loud enough to hear ourselves
and believe our own words....

—Christine Craig from "Poem"

EDMONIA LEWIS
(1843–1890)

Daughter of a Chippewa mother and a Black father, Lewis was a sculptor whose heritage greatly influenced her work. Orphaned before age five, she was raised with the name Wildfire by her mother's tribe. When she enrolled at Oberlin College with financial support from her brother, she changed her name. In 1862, Lewis moved to Boston and began her career as a sculptor with statues of leaders of the anti-slavery movement. The sale of her work enabled her to go to Italy in 1865 to further her study and gain access to cheap marble. Although working in the Neoclassic style, her art expressed her concern with slavery and racial oppression, reflected the dignity of her Indian roots, and, as she put it, conveyed a "strong sympathy for all women who have struggled and suffered." She was welcomed in Rome and was part of the circle of independent women artists that included Harriet Hosmer, Charlotte Cushman, and Anne Whitney. Though she confronted racial and sexual barriers, Lewis attained professional success both in the United States and Europe.

FEBRUARY

18 In 1975, **Darlene Hayes** became an associate producer on the "Phil Donahue Show."

Author, professor, and Nobel Peace Prize winner **Toni Morrison** was born on this day in 1931. *(See also March 31.)*

Taytu Betul, empress of Ethiopia, **19** gave the name Addis Ababa to the new capital. Taytu Betul was the wife of King Menilek II during his reign (1889–1913). She died during this month in 1918.

20 Jazz vocalist **Nancy Wilson** was born on this day in 1937.

The "High Priestess of Soul," **Nina Simone**, **21** was born Eunice Kathleen Waymon on this day in 1933.

FEBRUARY

22 In 1976, **Barbara Jordan** became the first Black and the first woman to make a keynote speech before the Democratic National Convention. In 1966, she was the first Black Texan since 1883 to be elected to the state senate. In 1972, she was elected to the U.S. House of Representatives. She also made the keynote speech to the Democratic National Convention in 1992. She was born this month in 1936.

In the 1920s, **Madame C. B. Reed** may have been the first Black woman to open her own business in the New York shopping district. She primarily made gowns for the wealthy during her 16 years in business. **23**

24 In 1919, **Ada S. McKinley** (1868–1952) founded the Southside Settlement House in Chicago for the poor.

Adrienne Mitchell became the first Black woman to die in combat in 1991 in the Persian Gulf War. **25**

FEBRUARY

26 Physical chemist **Johnnie H. Watts** (born in 1922) is one of the few Black women scientists frequently published in scientific journals.

World class figure skater **Debi Thomas** became the first Black to ever win a medal in the Winter Olympics on this day in 1988. **27**

Τrue emancipation lies in the acceptance of the whole past, in deriving strength from all my roots.

—Pauli Murray

Photo by Elizabeth Williams

Woman, instead of being elevated by her union with man, which might be expected from an alliance with a superior being, is in reality lowered. She generally loses her individuality, her independent character, her moral being. She becomes absorbed into him, and henceforth is looked at and acts through the medium of her husband.

—Sarah Moore Grimke (1792–1873)
from a September 1837 letter

FEBRUARY/MARCH

28 **Phoebe Francis**, owner of the Francis Tavern, saved General George Washington's life during the Revolutionary War by exposing a plot to poison him.

Hattie McDaniel became the first Black to receive an Academy Award on this day in 1940 for her role in *Gone With The Wind*. **29**

1 On this day in 1864, the first Black women physicians, **Rebecca Lee, Rebecca Cole**, and **Susan McKinney**, graduated from the New England Female Medical College.

Prima ballerina **Janet Collins** became the first Black to perform on the stage of the Metropolitan Opera House in 1951 by dancing in *Aida*. She was born on this day in 1917. **2**

MARCH

3 The world's best woman athlete, **Jackie Joyner-Kersee**, was born on this day in 1962. In the 1988 Olympics, she set records in the heptathlon and the long jump.

4 Internationally acclaimed South African folksinger **Miriam Makeba** was born on this day in 1932.

5 In 1984, **Leontine Kelly** became the first Black woman bishop of the United Methodist Church. She was born on this day in 1920.

6 **Queen Charlotte Sophia** (1744–1818) was the wife of King George III of England, the grandmother of Queen Victoria, and the great-great-grandmother of George VI.

...we need to feel the cheer and inspiration of meeting each other, we need to gain the courage and fresh life that comes from the mingling of congenial souls, of those working for the same ends. Next, we need to talk over not only those things which are of vital importance to us as women, but also the things that are of especial interest to us as *colored* women.

—Josephine St. Pierre Ruffin (1842–1924), founded the New Era Club, which issued *The Women's Era* newspaper, which she edited. This grew into the National Federation of Afro-American Women in 1895.

Words are easy, friendship hard.

—Ganda (Uganda) proverb—Gikuyu proverb

Photo by Elizabeth Williams

Mere feminine, delicate, Dresden china type of women get nowhere in business or professional life. They marry millionaires, if they are lucky. But if a woman is to make headway with men, she must be truly masculine.

—Jessie Tarbox Beals (1870–1942)
quoted in *Jessie Tarbox Beals: First Woman News Photographer*,
by Alexander Alland (1978)

MARCH

7 **Eulalie Spence**, one of only a few female playwrights prior to the 1950s, died in 1981. Her only full-length play, *The Whipping*, a comedy, was sold to Paramount Pictures but was never produced.

Phyllis Mae Daley was the first Black nurse in the Navy. Along with **Helen Turner, Ella Lucille Stimley**, and **Edith DeVoe**, she served on active duty during World War II. **8**

9 **Whoopi Goldberg** became the second Black woman to win an Oscar, for her role in *Ghost*. *(See also November 13.)*

"Black Moses" **Harriet Tubman** died **10** of pneumonia on this day in 1913. She made at least 15 trips into the South to rescue more than 200 slaves and deliver them to freedom through the Underground Railroad. *(See also April 20.)*

MARCH

11 *A Raisin in the Sun*, a play by **Lorraine Hansberry**, opened at the Ethel Barrymore Theatre in New York City on this day in 1959. This was the first play by a Black woman to be produced on Broadway.

Virginia Hamilton, award-winning author of books for children and adolescents, was born on this day in 1936. **12**

13 In 1990, **Elaine Waddington** was named assistant general manager of the Boston Red Sox.

During the 1970s, **Audrey Weaver** became the first Black woman to hold the position of managing editor of a daily newspaper, the *Chicago Daily Defender*. **14**

MARCH

15 Activist **Fanny Lou Hamer**, the first Black woman from Mississippi to run for Congress (in 1964), died on this day from diabetes, heart trouble, and breast cancer. *(See also October 6.)*

In 1977, **Dr. Carolyn Payton** became the first woman director of the Peace Corps. **16**

...being of one body yet sharing many voices is the daily life and strength of black women.

—Julia A. Boyd

MARIAN ANDERSON
(B. 1902)

Born in Philadelphia,
Pennsylvania, Anderson grew
up with a joy for music that
made singing as natural to her
as speaking. Although her
family encouraged her, and
her high school principal
introduced her to Boghetti,
her vocal coach, Anderson felt
that opera was a world closed
to her. She persevered in spite
of this and became the first
Black woman to sing at the
Metropolitan Opera, in 1955,
in the role of Ulrica in Verdi's
Un Ballo in Maschera. She sang
seven performances. The event
was of such significance in the
history of race relations that
The New York Times ran a
front-page story after the first
performance. She went on to
be appointed U.S. delegate to
the United Nations from 1958
to 1959. She received the
Presidential Medal of Freedom
in 1963.

MARCH

17   **Thelma E. Berlack**, the first Black woman admitted to Delta Mu Delta (journalism's equivalent to Phi Beta Kappa), was born in 1906. She was one of the few Black women writing about New York City society in the 1920s.

In 1977, **Unita Blackwell** was elected Mississippi's first Black woman mayor, of Mayersville, Mississippi. She was born on this day in 1933. **18**

19   During this month in 1977, **Alexia Herman**, just 29 years old, became the youngest director of the Women's Bureau in the U.S. Department of Labor's 57-year history.

Ruth Lowery started a mid-eighteenth century silk industry in Huntsville, Alabama. The silks she produced surpassed Asiatic and European silks at international fairs. Abolition-ists would not buy imported silks because they were made by child labor. Ruth Lowery's mill filled this need. **20**

MARCH

21 On this day in 1960, the two-day **Sharpeville Massacre** began in South Africa. Hundreds of unarmed protesters against the pass-book laws stood silently outside the police station in Sharpeville, a Black township. The police opened fire on the group and within 40 seconds, 69 people lay dead.

Today also marks the anniversary of the 1965 **Selma Freedom March**.

During 1969–1970, **Tina Sloane-Green** became the first Black woman to compete on the U.S. National Lacrosse team. **22**

23 Four-time Grammy winning rock vocalist **Chaka Khan** was born Yvette Marie Stevens on this day in 1953.

Dorothy Height, the president of the National Council of Negro Women, was born on this day in 1912. **24**

...black women are more
often visualized in mainstream
American culture—most
prominently as fashion models
or as performers in music
videos—than they are allowed
to speak their own words, or
speak about their condition....

—Michelle Wallace

Why must it be assumed that
we necessarily have to get our
images of ourselves through our
contacts with white Americans,
when we have each other (blacks)
with whom to identify?

—Lena Wright Myers

ZORA NEALE HURSTON
(1907–1960)

Zora Neale Hurston began her writing career in high school in Jacksonville, Florida. She wrote her first short story for Stylus at Barnard College where she received a B.A. Although she had a scholarship, Hurston worked as a maid and manicurist to support herself in New York City. Upon receiving her degree she became Fannie Hurst's secretary. She received a private grant from Mrs. R. Osgood Mason and a fellowship from the Rosenwald Foundation, which enabled her to study anthropology and folk-lore at Columbia University. She traveled and lived in the British West Indies on a Guggenheim Fellowship, studying folklore from 1936 to 1938. Hurston also produced programs of Negro spirituals and work songs that she took on the road to St. Louis. She worked a while for Paramount Studios and Warner Brothers in Hollywood and also held a position as librarian at the Library of Congress. Hurston's works were intricately linked with the Harlem Renaissance. She returned to Florida in the mid-1940s. At the time of her stroke and subsequent death, she was working on her last novel, *The Life of Herod the Great*.

MARCH

25 "Queen of Soul" **Aretha Franklin** was born on this day in 1942. She was the first female singer to earn five gold records.

"The Divine One," jazz vocalist **Sarah Vaughn**, was born on this day in 1924. **26**

Diana Ross, pop vocalist, actress, and model, was also born on this day, in 1944.

27 Playwright, composer, designer, and director **Shirley Graham** died on this day in 1977. She was one of only a few Black women prior to the 1950s to pursue a career in professional theater. She also was the founding editor of *Freedomways Magazine* in 1960.

Writer **Toni Cade Bambara** was born during this month in 1939. She also edited *The Black Woman: An Anthology*, the first of its kind in the United States. Published in 1970, it is now recognized as beginning the twentieth-century renaissance of Black women's literature. **28**

MARCH/APRIL

29 Actress and comedienne **Pearl Bailey** was born on this day in 1918.

30 In 1989, **Euzham Palcy** became the first Black woman director of a full-length film, *A Dry White Season*.

Fashion model and executive **Naomi Sims** was born on this day in 1948.

31 *Beloved* won **Toni Morrison** the Pulitzer Prize for literature on this day in 1988. *(See also February 18.)*

1 **Juanita Hall** (1901–1968) created the role of Bloody Mary in the 1950 Broadway musical *South Pacific*. She was awarded the prestigious Donaldson Award for her supporting performance.

APRIL

2 In 1976, **Janie Mines** became the first Black female to enter the U.S. Naval Academy in the 131-year history of Annapolis. When women were admitted for the first time in 1976, she was the only Black. She was the first Black woman to graduate and was assigned to the Naval Training Center in Orlando, Florida. Her sister Gwen entered in 1977 and graduated in 1981!

Lelia K. Smith Foley **3** was elected mayor of Taft, Oklahoma, in 1973. She is believed to be the first Black woman mayor in the continental United States.

To be a Black woman...is not just to be a Black who happens to be a woman, for one discovers one's sex sometime before one discovers one's racial classification.

—Kay Lindsey

BESSIE SMITH
(1894–1937)

Born in Chattanooga, Tennessee, Bessie Smith began performing in minstrel shows with her brother, until she became a leading performer on the TOBA (known as "Tough on Black Asses") circuit and at the 81 Theater in Atlanta. Her first recording, "Down-hearted Blues," established her as the most successful Black performing artist of her day. She recorded with jazz greats Charlie Green, Joe Smith, and Louis Armstrong. In 1929, she appeared in the film *St. Louis Blues.* The Great Depression, as well as her alcoholism, affected her career, but by 1933 she was recording again because of the increasing demand of European audiences for jazz recordings. Smith's last recording featured jazz greats Benny Goodman and Jack Teagarden. Smith died of injuries sustained in a car accident. Smith's work has been recorded by other jazz women, such as Dinah Washington, Lavern Baker, and Juanita Hall.

APRIL

4 The poet, writer, actress, and composer **Maya Angelou** was born on this day in 1928. *(See also January 20.)*

5 **Johnnetta Betsch Cole** was named the first Black woman president of Spelman College in Atlanta, Georgia, in 1987.

6 **Jill Brown** received her wings and became a first officer with Texas International Airlines in 1978, thus becoming the first Black woman pilot with a major scheduled airline.

7 "Lady Day," **Billie Holiday**—perhaps the greatest of all jazz singers—was born Eleanor Fagan on this day in 1917.

APRIL

8 Equal rights activist **Eleanor Holmes Norton** was born on this day in 1938. She was appointed the first female chair of the Equal Employment Opportunity Commission (EEOC) by President Jimmy Carter in 1977.

The great American contralto **Marian Anderson** sang at the Lincoln Memorial on this day in 1939. *(See also January 7.)* **9**

10 **Johnnie Tillmon**, the founder of the National Welfare Rights Organization, was born on this day in 1926.

Dr. Justina Ford, who in 1902 was the first Black female doctor in Colorado, died in Denver in 1952 at age 81. **11**

When a woman, and certainly a Black woman, won't act like a Negro, a Lady and a martyr Christian, she usually gets labeled a bitch. A woman is a bitch if she stands up for herself, speaks her mind, insists on her rights and space, is not deferential to man and would rather make a scene than die or turn the other cheek.

—Judy Simmons

What I am is a humanist before any-thing—before I'm a Jew, before I'm black, before I'm a woman. And my beliefs are for the human race—they don't exclude any-one. But somehow we are supposed to be credits to our race. The mere fact that I'm still around makes me a credit to my race, which is the human race.

—Whoopi Goldberg

BILLIE HOLIDAY
(1915–1959)

Billie Holiday was born Eleanora Fagan in Baltimore. Abandoned by her father at an early age, she had no contact with him until after her first success. Holiday was left by her mother in the care of family members who mistreated her; she rejoined her mother in New York in 1928. She began singing at a club in Brooklyn and moved up steadily until discovered by John Hammond in 1933. Her first three recording sessions were with Benny Goodman. From there, "Lady Day" recorded regularly with Lester Young and Teddy Wilson. By 1937 Holiday had joined Count Basie, and in 1938 she became one of the first Black singers to perform with white band leader Artie Shaw. Her popularity landed her a part in the film *New Orleans* with Louis Armstrong and Kid Ory. However, her abuse of alcohol and hard drugs, as well as her attachment to men who mistreated her, caused her not only to lose her income, but also her spirit. Holiday is considered not just a jazz singer, but a woman who, by virtue of her unique and widely imitated vocal phrasings, made a mark on the jazz idiom itself.

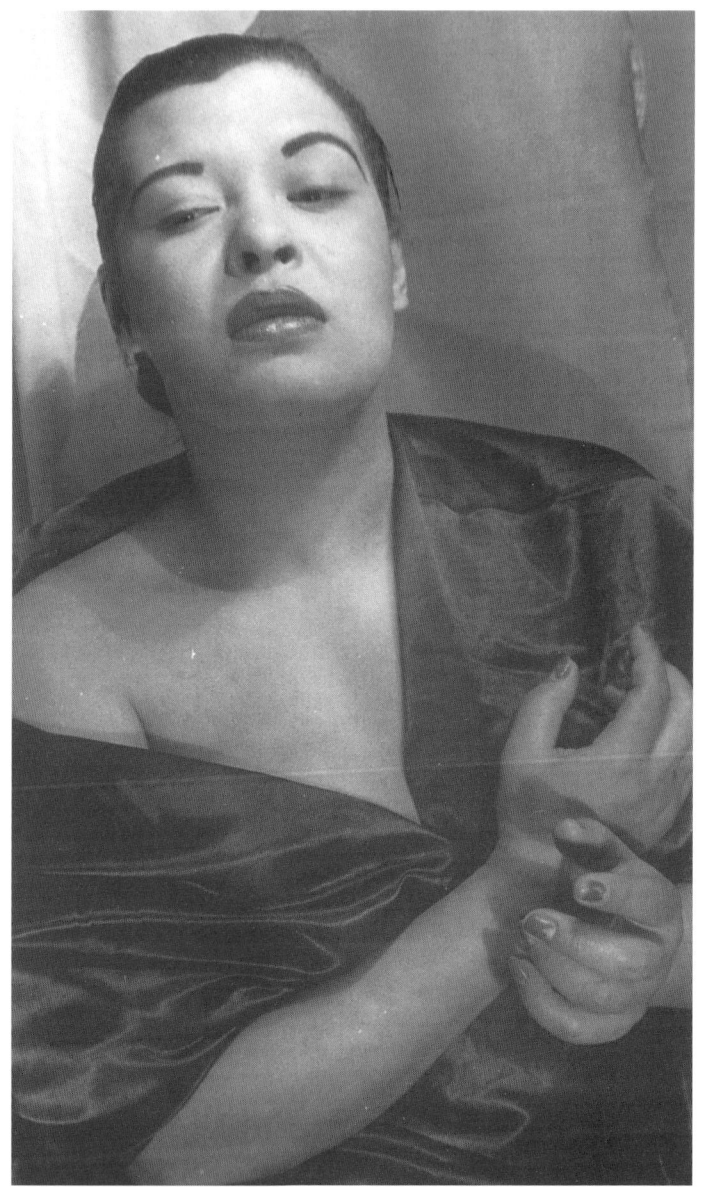

APRIL

12 In 1921, **Mayme Diggs** and her husband founded Michigan's largest Black funeral home in Detroit.

In 1939, **Mary T. Washington** became **13** the first Black woman certified public accountant.

14 *Bright Road*, released in 1953, gained **Mary Elizabeth Vroman** (1923–1967) entry into the Screenwriters Guild, making her the first Black woman granted guild membership.

Norma Merrick Sklarek, the first **15** Black woman licensed architect in New York and California, was born on this day in 1928.

APRIL

16 In 1947, biological chemist **Marie Maynard Daly** (born in 1921) became the first Black woman to earn a Ph.D. in chemistry from Columbia University.

Althea T. L. Simmons, the chief congressional lobbyist of the National Association for the Advancement of Colored People (NAACP), was born on this day in 1924. **17**

18 In 1937, **Willa Brown** became the first Black woman commercial pilot to earn a license.

On this day in 1972, **Mikki Grant's** Broadway hit musical *Don't Bother Me I Can't Cope* opened in New York City. **19**

APRIL

20 In 1853, **Harriet Tubman** (born in the 1820s) started the Underground Railroad. *(See also March 10.)*

In 1971, the **Honorable C. Delores Tucker** became the first Black woman Secretary of State appointed to the cabinet of the Commonwealth of Pennsylvania. **21**

Let us begin to recognize the wonderful continuum involved in being unabashedly and excitingly and intensely female. Let us affirm this woman in the world and in ourselves.

—Sabring Sojourner

DINAH WASHINGTON
(1924–1963)

Born Ruth Lee Jones in Tuscaloosa, Alabama, Washington's style was deeply influenced by her experience as a singer and pianist for Sallie Martin's gospel choir in Chicago. She was given the name Dinah Washington by the manager of the Garrick Stage Bar, where she was discovered by Lionel Hampton. She performed with Hampton's band from 1943 to 1946, then enjoyed a successful solo recording career from 1946 to 1959, reworking popular country, blues, pop, and R&B standards. Her breakthrough hit, "What a Difference a Day Makes" (1959), marked her entrance into the general pop market, where she earned several more gold records. She died in Detroit due to an accidental overdose of sleeping pills.

APRIL

22 In 1988, **Martha Bibb** reached the top of Michigan's civil service and became the first Black woman to be director of personnel for the State of Michigan.

The **National Council of Negro Women** was founded in 1935. **23**

24 In 1967, jazz vocalist **Doris Banks** became the first Black in Baltimore to own a fur business.

The great jazz vocalist **Ella Fitzgerald** was born on this day in 1918. **25**

APRIL

26 In 1892, **Sarah Boone** received a patent for an ironing board with smooth, curved edges.

27 In 1969, **Coretta Scott King** became the first woman of any race to preach at Saint Paul's Cathedral in London, England. She was born on this day in 1927.

28 In 1782, **Deborah Gannett** enlisted as Robert Shurtleff in the Fourth Massachusetts Regiment during the American Revolutionary War and served to the end of the war. She was later honored by the Massachusetts State Legislature for heroism.

29 Sculptor **Selma H. Burke** created the portrait of Franklin D. Roosevelt that is used on the U.S. dime.

When I was a little girl my grandmother—
who was in her early seventies—would say:
"Child you're black and you are going to
be a woman and I don't think you can
change either one of the two. But you are
bright and you have a brain. Use it to
show them you are coming through.

—Shirley Chisholm

The dread inspired by the growing intelligence of colored women has interested us
almost to the point of amusement. It has
given to the colored women a new sense
of importance to witness how easily their
emancipation and steady advancement is
disturbing all classes of American people.

—Fannie Barrier Williams

SARAH VAUGHN
(1924–1995)

Born Sarah Lois Vaughn, "Sassy," as she was known to her family, began her performing career as a choir member and organist for Mount Zion Baptist Church in Newark, New Jersey. In 1924, she won an amateur contest at the Apollo Theater in Harlem and shortly afterwards joined pianist Earl Hines' big band as a second pianist and second singer to Billy Eckstine. Her later work with Eckstine's bop-oriented big band led to her association with jazz legends Dizzy Gillespie and Charlie Parker, with whom she recorded "Lover Man" in 1945. She recorded on such labels as Roulette, Mercury, and Columbia. Her contralto voice was capable of wide leaps, which made improvisations ranging from crystal clarity to a blues-influenced growl sound simple. When Sarah Vaughn died, she left behind a discography dating from 1944 to 1987.

APRIL/MAY

30 **Gloria Scott** was elected national president of the Girl Scouts in 1975 and became the first Black woman in that position.

In 1949, **Evelyn Boyd Collins** (born in 1924) received her Ph.D. in mathematics from Yale University, becoming the first Black woman to achieve an advanced degree in this field from Yale. **1**

2 With the publication of her short story "The Two Officers" (1852) and her novel *Iola Leroy* in 1892, **Frances E. W. Harper** became the first Black woman to have a short story and a novel published.

In 1886, the **Alpha Home for Aged Colored Women**—perhaps the first of such home for Black women—opened in Indiana. **3**

MAY

4 Emmy Award-winning journalist and a regular contributor on "The MacNeil Lehrer News Hour," **Charlayne Hunter-Gault** was born in 1942. She was one of two Black students to desegregate the University of Georgia, Athens, in 1961.

5 The U.S. Navy (Waves) admitted Black women in 1944.

6 Distinguished surgeon **Dr. Dorothy L. Brown**, who was reared in an orphanage and then by foster parents, became Meharry Medical College's first woman graduate in 1948.

7 **Josephine Ruffin** edited the first Black woman's newspaper, *The Women's Era*, which was started in 1894. This paper was the monthly journal of the New Era Club, a group organized to keep Black women's clubs aware of each other's activities. *The Women's Era* was published until 1903.

MAY

8   Jazz pianist and innovative composer **Mary Lou Williams** was born on this day in 1910.

Florence Beatrice Smith Price, the first Black woman recognized as an award-winning composer, had one of her symphonies performed at the Chicago World's Fair by the Chicago Symphony in 1933.   **9**

... black women must speak in a plurality of voices as well as in a multiplicity of discourses.

—Mae Gwendolyn Henderson

MARY LOU WILLIAMS
(1910–1981)

Originally named Mary Elfrieda Scruggs, pianist-composer Williams began performing professionally early in her life in Pittsburgh. She was known as Mary Lou Burley until 1925, when she joined John Williams' group and married him. In 1929, Williams served as pianist and arranger for Andy Kirk's Twelve Clouds of Joy. Her arrangements led band leaders such as Earl Hines, Tommy Dorsey, and Benny Goodman to commission Williams' swing-band scores. In 1942, Williams formed her own group with her second husband, Shorty Baker, and briefly worked as staff arranger for Duke Ellington, writing for him the well-known "Trumpet No End" in 1946. Williams also was an important figure in New York bop, contributing scores to Dizzy Gillespie's big band. She remained active through the seventies and, besides her jazz compositions, wrote sacred works such as *Black Christ of the Andes* (1963) and *Mary Lou's Mass* (1970), which was choreographed by Alvin Ailey.

MAY

10 In 1854, "The Black Swan," **Elizabeth Taylor Greenfield**, a gifted vocalist with a 27-note range, performed at Buckingham Palace for Queen Victoria.

In 1979, **Amayla Kearse** became the first woman named to the U.S. Appeals Court in New York State, one of the most important commercial courts in the country. **11**

12 **Maida Springer Kemp**, trade union movement advocate and organizer in 1933 and for many years afterward, was born on this day in 1910.

Francis Ann Rollins, using the pseudonym Frank A. Rollins, published *The Life and Public Services of Martin R. Delany*, the first biography of a free-born Black man. **13**

MAY

14 In 1868, **Fannie Moore Richards** became the first Black schoolteacher in Detroit, Michigan.

Clara Brown, the "Angel of the Rockies" in the early eighteenth century, was a former slave from Kentucky who became the owner of several gold mines. She was then able to buy many of her friends and relatives out of slavery in Kentucky. She secured her own freedom at age 55. She also sponsored two trains of Black families traveling from Leavenworth, Kansas, to Colorado. She was buried with honors by the Colorado Pioneer Association. **15**

16 In 1953, **Toni Stone**, age 22, signed to play professional baseball with the champion Indianapolis Clowns, a Negro American League team. By the time she played with them her batting average was .265. She played second base.

Although she could neither read nor write, **Lillian Harris** amassed a fortune in real estate in the early part of the twentieth century before she died in 1928. **17**

It was a pleasantly warm evening in Cincinnati, in the year 1853, and the lecture hall was thronged with people who had come to hear the famous platform speaker, Sojourner Truth, expound on her favorite subject, the Abolitionist movement. When she had finished her lecture, a Southerner who was in full accord with the concept of slavery, approached her and, sneering, commented, "You were wrong in everything you said. Why, without slavery, the Negroes would starve to death. They were *made* to be slaves. As far as I am concerned, you made no more impression than a flea-bite."

"I am sorry to hear that," replied Sojourner Truth sweetly, "but perhaps, with God's help, I can keep you scratching!"

ELLA FITZGERALD
(B. 1918)

Born in Newport News, Virginia, Fitzgerald was orphaned in early childhood. She moved to New York City and attended an orphanage school in Yonkers. Like many young Black performers, she was discovered at a contest sponsored by Harlem's Apollo Theater. This led to her engagement with Chick Webb's band during the Swing Era. From 1939 to 1942 she led that band, then embarked on a solo career. In 1956, she severed her connection with Decca Records and moved to Verve, where, with arranger and orchestra leader Nelson Riddle, she recorded a series of "songbooks" dedicated to American songwriters. From there she made frequent appearances with Oscar Peterson, Count Basie, and guitarist Joe Pass, to name just a few. Her voice was admired by Charlie Parker because of her range and her improvised scat solos. Her gift of vocal mimicry has earned her the devotion of fans of all ages and influenced American musicians, as well as international performers such as Miriam Makeba.

MAY

18 The first Black and the youngest person ever chosen, **Rita Dove** at age 40 was named the U.S. poet laureate on this day in 1993.

In 1970, **Gwendolyn B. Cherry** became the first Black woman elected to the Florida legislature. **19**

20 Only the third woman in history designated as one of the "Ten Most Wanted," political activist, professor, scholar, and writer Angela Y. Davis was arrested by FBI agents in New York City in 1970. She was later acquitted of all charges. *(See also January 26)*

When she was employed by Mohawk Airlines in 1958, **Ruth Carol Taylor** became America's first Black flight attendant. **21**

MAY

22 Singer, actress, and performer **Lena Horne** (born 1917) opened her one-woman show (*Lena Horne: The Lady and Her Music*) on Broadway during this month in 1981. She received a special Tony Award for her performance.

In 1981, **Delores Anderson Davis** (born in 1933) was the only Black gerontologist in the United States. **23**

24 **Martha B. Goldman** may have become the first Black woman to work in a secretarial capacity for the federal government in 1918, at the Bureau of Standards.

One of the first Black women millionaires, **Madame C. J. Walker** (Sarah Breedlove), inventor of a straightening comb for Black women, died on this day in 1919. **25**

Today is **African Liberation Day**.

It was this peaceful world of black people simply dreaming in their own skins that I began to slowly absorb into my own life. It was like finding black power and black personality in a simple and natural way.

—Bessie Head

Down through the ages, the image of majesty have come to the black girl in the admonition: "Walk proud! You are the descendant of queens!"

—Jeanne Noble

When it comes to the cause of justice, I take no prisoners and I don't believe in compromising.

—Mary Frances Berry

MARY FIELDS
(1832–1914)

Known also as "Stagecoach Mary," Fields was a Montana pioneer and the second woman stagecoach driver on a U.S. mail route. Proud, independent, over 6 feet tall, and handy with a shotgun, Fields was born a slave in Tennessee but escaped to Toledo, Ohio, where she became a general handywoman at an Ursuline convent. After her close friend Mother Amadeus and other nuns left to start a mission school for Native American girls near Cascade, Montana, Fields soon followed, resuming her old job and becoming the nuns' protector. When one of the mission's hired hands crossed her, she fired bullets past his ears and sent him hightailing across the plains. Many other colorful tales added to Fields's legend. She worked as a servant, nurse, restaurateur, and freight-hauler. She held her postal job for eight years, becoming a fixture along the trail, driving two teams of horses and smoking big cigars. She is remembered not only for her zestful life, but also for her kindness and eagerness to help others.

MAY

26 Author of *Behind the Scenes or Thirty Years a Slave and Four Years in the White House*, **Elizabeth Keckley**, seamstress for both Mrs. Jefferson Davis and Mary Todd Lincoln, died on this day in 1907.

In 1963, the **Clara Ward Singers** were the first gospel group to sing in Radio City Music Hall in New York City. **27**

28 Vocalist **Gladys Knight** was born on this day in 1944.

In 1963, **Katherine Dunham** (born in 1910) became the first Black choreographer to work at the New York Metropolitan Opera House. **29**

MAY/JUNE

30 Despite being totally blind, dramatic soprano **Marie Luvenia Fitzhugh** became a prima donna in 1905. She sang in three languages, played piano, and was able to sew and knit.

Born Lauretta Aiken, comedienne **Jackie "Moms" Mabley** died this month in 1975. **31**

1 **Sojourner Truth** left New York to begin her travels as an antislavery activist on this day in 1843. *(See also November 26.)*

Dorothy West, a novelist during the Harlem Renaissance of the 1920s, was born on this day in 1907. **2**

The baby-doll type of woman is a thing of the past, and the wide-awake woman is forging ahead prepared for all emergencies, and ready to answer any call, even if it be to face the cannons on the battlefield.

—Amy-Jacques Garvey

Now that you have touched the women, you have struck a rock, you have dislodged a boulder, and you will be crushed.

—chant by South African women during the 1956 campaign against pass laws

HARRIET TUBMAN
(1820–1913)

Tubman is the best-known "conductor" to have worked on the Underground Railroad, a network of abolitionists who undermined slavery by spiriting Blacks to freedom in the North and Canada. A fugitive herself (from Maryland to Philadelphia in 1849), she risked many return trips to rescue some 300 slaves. Rewards for her capture totaled $40,000. Her courage and shrewdness were remarkable considering that she suffered recurrent blackouts from a concussion she received at age thirteen, when an overseer struck her on the head with a two-pound weight. During the Civil War, Tubman served the Union as a nurse, spy, and commander of small groups of male scouts engaged in raiding parties behind Confederate lines. Congress recognized this work by awarding her a pension. Tubman spent the rest of her life near Auburn, New York, establishing a home for indigent aged Blacks, promoting schools for freed Blacks in the South, taking a leading role in the growth of the A.M.E. Church in upstate New York, and working in the Black suffrage movement.

JUNE

3 World renowned U.S. dancer **Josephine Baker** was born on this day in 1906. Picasso is reported to have said, "She is the Nefertiti of now."

4 Entomologist **Vivian Chambers** was born on this day in 1903. She received her Ph.D. at Cornell University in 1946 and became a senior researcher at the American Museum of Natural History.

5 In 1973, **Doris A. Davis** was elected mayor of Compton, California, becoming the first Black woman to govern a metropolitan city.

6 **Marian Wright Edelman**, the founder of the Children's Defense Fund in 1973 and the first Black woman admitted to the Mississippi bar in 1965, was born on this day in 1939.

JUNE

7 Pulitzer Prize poet **Gwendolyn Brooks** was born on this day in 1917.

Poet **Nikki Giovanni** was also born on this day in 1943.

Mary Fields, perhaps born in 1832, was the second woman to drive a stagecoach and deliver the U.S. mail. While in her 60s, she drove the Cascade, Montana, route. She died in 1914. **8**

9 Billed as the "Black Garbo" in Europe in the 1930s and the first Black actress credited on the screen, **Nina Mae McKinney** starred at Metro-Goldwyn-Mayer in Hollywood.

During this month in 1918, **Frances Elliot** became the first Black nurse in the Red Cross. **10**

JUNE

11 On this day in 1963, **Vivian Malone**, escorted by federal National Guard troops, enrolled at the University of Alabama despite opposition by Governor George Wallace.

In 1976, **Addie Wyatt** became the first woman vice-president elected to the International Executive Board of the Amalgamated Meat Cutters and Butcher Workmen of North America (AFL-CIO). **12**

It's essential that we understand that taking care of the planet will be done *as* we take care of ourselves. You know that you can't really make much of a difference in things until you change yourself.

—Alice Walker

Photo courtesy of Smithsonian Institution

"Now that things are turning and many are opening their eyes to what I've tried to do and desiring to have a share in the same, the question in my heart and mind, and God only knows how it hurts, is just what are they going to ask me to submit as a Negro woman to get their interest, for there are some men who occupy high places who feel that no Negro woman, whether she be cook, criminal, or principal of a school, should ever be addressed as Mrs."

—Charlotte Brown (1882–1961)
letter to F. P. Hobgood, Jr. (1921)

JUNE

13 When named assistant coach to the University of Kentucky men's basketball team in 1990, **Bernadette Locke** became the first woman on-court coach.

14 In 1939, **Ethel Waters** became the first Black woman to star in a Broadway drama. She played the lead role in *Mamba's Daughters* and received seventeen curtain calls on opening night.

15 In 1971, **Cheryl White** became the first Black female jockey.

16 When **Cheryl A. Brown** won the Miss Iowa title in 1970, she became the first Black to compete in a Miss America beauty pageant.

Marita Bonner was born this day in 1899. *(See also October 25.)*

JUNE

17 **Azie Taylor Morton**, the thirty-sixth Treasurer of the United States, was the first Black woman to hold this position. Her signature appeared on $1, $5, and $10 bills.

In 1909, **Nannie Burroughs** founded the National Training School for Women. **18**

19 Actress **Phylicia Rashad**, the mother on the "Bill Cosby Show," was born on this day in 1949.

Today is **Juneteenth National Freedom Day**. This celebrated statewide Texas holiday commemorates the day that word of the official end of the Civil War reached Galveston, through the efforts of Union soldiers.

In 1985, **Lynette Woodward** became the first woman to play basketball with the Harlem Globetrotters. **20**

If there is a single distinguishing feature of the literature of black women—and this accounts for their lack of recognition—it is this: their literature is about black women; it takes the trouble to record the thoughts, words, feelings, and deeds of black women, experiences that make the realities of being black in America look very different from what men have written.

—Mary Helen Washington, one of the pioneers
in Black women's literary tradition

It might be said that the genuine poetry of the black women appeared not in literature (during the Harlem Renaissance) but in the lyrics of blues singers like Bessie Smith. Female blues singers…wrote about the black woman's autonomy and vulnerability, sexuality and spirituality.

—Barbara Christian

"True chivalry respects all womanhood....Virtue knows no color lines, and the chivalry which depends upon complexion of skin and texture of hair can command no honest respect."

—Ida B. Wells (1862–1931)
A Red Record (1895)

JUNE

21 **Ann Allen Shockley**, author, researcher, and librarian at Fisk University, was born on this day in 1927.

Octavia Butler, speculative fiction writer and Hugo Award winner for excellence in science fiction in 1984 and 1985, was born on this day in 1947. **22**

23 A former polio victim, **Wilma G. Rudolph** became the first U.S. woman to win three gold medals in a single Olympiad during the 1960 Olympics in Rome, Italy. She was born on this day in 1940.

In 1841, *Essays: Including Biographies and Miscellaneous Pieces in Prose and Poetry* by **Ann Plato** was the first book of essays published by a Black. It was reprinted in 1988. **24**

JUNE

25 **Nettie Elizabeth Mills** was the first woman to own and operate an oil-drilling rig.

Jamaica Kincaid became a literary celebrity when the *New Yorker* magazine published her single-sentence, two-page short story, "Girl," which appeared on this day in 1978. **26**

27 **Ruth White**, at age 18, became the first Black and youngest woman to ever win a national fencing championship. In 1969, she held four national titles.

Mary McLeod Bethune, founder and president of Bethune-Cookman College in Florida, received the Spingarn Medal from the NAACP on this day in 1935. **28**

JUNE

29 **Catherine Ferguson** (1744–1854), believed to be the first Black woman teacher in America, opened Cathy Ferguson's School for the Poor in New York City in 1793.

In 1978, **Reverend Joan Martin** became the first Black woman to be ordained in the United Presbyterian Church. **30**

I have always felt that one great advantage of being both Black and a woman was that I started off with nothing to lose.

—Naomi Sims

"They had had the privilege of growing up where they'd raised a lot of food. They were never hungry. They could share their food with people. And so, you share your lives with people."

—Ella Baker (1903–1986)
quoted by Ellen Cantarow in *Moving the Mountain* (1980)

JULY

1 **Berthel Carmichael**, research mathematician, was the first Black woman to go to sea on a military oceanographic research ship. Since 1947 she worked as a crewmember of the U.S.S. Hayes. She performed computations that aid oceanographers in understanding underwater currents.

2 The first permanent order of Black Catholic nuns, the **Oblate Sisters of Providence**, was founded in Baltimore on this day in 1829.

3 In 1977, **Donna Lynn Mosley** became the first Black to compete in the U.S. Gymnastics Federation Junior Olympic Nationals.

4 **Edmonia Lewis**, born on this day in 1845, was the first Black to receive critical recognition as a sculptor.

JULY

5 In 1954, **Anna Arnold Hedgeman** became the first woman to serve in the cabinet of a New York City mayor, Robert F. Wagner. She was born on this day in 1899.

In 1975, the **Freddye Scarborough Henderson** Travel Agency was the first in the United States to operate group tours to West Africa. She was also the first Black appointed to the U.S. Travel Service. **6**

7 **Althea Gibson** became the first Black to win the women's single tennis championship, in 1957, at Wimbledon, England.

In 1978, **Faye Wattleton** became the first Black woman president of Planned Parenthood Federation of America. She was born on this day in 1943. **8**

Your time is now, my sisters.... New goals and new priorities, not only for this country, but for all of mankind must be set. Formal education will not help us do that. We must therefore depend upon informal learning. We can do that by confronting people with their humanity and their own inhumanity—confronting them wherever we meet them: in the church, in the classroom, on the floor of the Congress and the state legislatures, in the bars, and on the streets. We must reject not only the stereotypes that others hold of us, but also the stereotypes that we hold of ourselves.

—Shirley Chisholm

"Where there is money, there is fighting."

> quoted in *Marian Anderson, a Portrait*, by Kosti Vehanen (1941)

"As long as you keep a person down, some part of you has to be down there to hold him down, so it means you cannot soar as you otherwise might."

> —Marion Anderson (b. 1902)
> interview on CBS-TV, December 30, 1957

JULY

9 Poet, prize-winning author, and professor **June Jordan** was born on this day in 1936.

10 In 1974, five Black women were among the first fifteen female cadets at the U.S. Merchant Marine Academy at Kings Point, New York.

11 On this day in 1958, **Daisy Bates** and the **Little Rock Nine** who desegregated Central High School in Little Rock, Arkansas, received the Spingarn Medal from the NAACP.

12 In 1891, **_The Creole Show_** in Boston was the first Black production to feature Black female singers.

JULY

13 The "Voudou Queen of New Orleans" for three generations, **Mademoiselle Marie LaVeau**, died in 1897.

Blues singer **Elizabeth "Libba" Cotten** died in 1987 at age 95. **14**

15 In 1968, **Ellen Holly** integrated daytime soap operas when she appeared on ABC's "One Life to Live."

The first Black female lawyer to practice before the U.S. Supreme Court, **Violette A. Johnson**, was born in 1882. **16**

JULY

17 During this month in 1977, **Janelle Commissiong** of Trinidad and Tobago became the first Black woman to win the Miss Universe title.

Jessie Redmond Fauset graduated from Cornell University in 1905. She was the first Black woman elected to the Phi Beta Kappa society. **18**

Women are blessed with a jewel of strength that glows all the time.

—Judith Jamison

Vaudeville performer

"All token blacks have the same experience. I have been pointed at as a solution to things that have not begun to be solved, because pointing at us token blacks eases the conscience of millions, and I think this is dreadfully wrong."

—Leontyne Price (b. 1927)
quoted in *Divas: Impressions of Six Opera Superstars*,
by Winthrop Sargeant (1959)

JULY

19 Journalist, anti-lynching advocate, and a founder of the NAACP, **Ida B. Wells** was born this month in 1862.

20 In 1942, 40 of the first 440 women who entered the Women's Army Auxiliary Corps (WAAC) and began training at Fort Des Moines (Iowa) were Black. *(See also December 2.)*

21 The **National Association of Colored Women** was founded by **Mary Church Terrell** in Washington, D.C., on this day in 1896.

22 In 1939, **Jane Bolin** was appointed the first Black woman judge in the United States.

JULY

23 **Vanessa Williams**, the first Black Miss America, relinquished her crown to the first runner-up, **Suzette Charles**, also Black, on this day in 1984.

During the late 1870s and 1880s, the California touring company, **The Hyers Sisters—Anna Maadah and Emma Louise Hyers**—staged a half-dozen plays and shows. **24**

25 **Anne Spencer**, a poet whose work predated the Harlem Renaissance of the 1920s and then contributed to it, died on this day in 1975.

In 1890, **Dr. Ida Gray**, a graduate of the University of Michigan, became the first Black woman to receive a degree in dentistry. **26**

We must begin to understand that a revolution entails not only the willingness to lay our lives on the firing line and get killed. In some ways, this is an easy commitment to make. To die for the revolution is a one-shot deal; to live for the revolution means taking on the more difficult commitment of changing our day-to-day patterns.

—Frances Beal

We need to uncover and (re)write our own multistoried history, and talk to one another as we are doing so.

—Gloria T. Hull

"Now the real beginnings of the "freedom," which we have discussed for many years—and a heady freedom it is, coming after so many years of reaching outward for it—to finally discover all I had to do was reach inward, and it was there waiting all the time for me!"

—Alisa Wills (b. 1929)
quoted in *The Woman's Eye* by Ann Tucker (1973)

JULY

27 The first Black woman in New England—and perhaps in the country—to broadcast a sustained radio program (from the mid-1950s until 1964), **Gretchen Flippen Jackson** was born in 1918.

28 In the 1890s, "America's most distinguished female baritone" was vaudeville performer **Hattie McIntosh**.

29 The first **National Convention (Conference) of Colored Women** was held in Boston, Massachusetts, in 1895.

30 **Sue Booker** (born in 1946) was the first Black woman to join the Directors Guild of America.

JULY/AUGUST

31 **Dr. Ruth Love** was the first woman and the first Black school superintendent in the Chicago school system.

1 On this day in 1876, **Mary Eliza Mahoney** became the first Black to graduate from a nursing school, the School of Nursing, New England Hospital for Women and Children, in Boston, Massachusetts.

The **National Bar Association** was formally organized by 12 Blacks, including **Gertrude E. Rush**, on this day in 1925.

2 **Jewell Jackson McCabe**, the president of the National Coalition of 100 Black Women, was born on this day in 1945. The coalition is a leadership forum that serves Black professional women, their communities, and provides mentors for youth. Each year the coalition presents the Candace Award honoring ten Black women in the arts, sciences, and business. The name is an Ethiopian term for "queen."

3 This month in 1974, **Beverly Johnson** became the first Black model to appear on the cover of *Vogue*.

AUGUST

4 **Aida Overton Walker** (1880–1914) was a successful singer and dancer featured in big shows and vaudeville.

Evelyn Ashford won the gold medal in the 100-meter race in the 1984 summer Olympics in Los Angeles, California. **5**

Physicist **Shirley Jackson** was born this day in 1946. In 1973, she was the first woman to receive a Ph.D. in particle physics from M.I.T. She's currently a theoretical physicist at Bell Laboratories.

I cannot change the world, but I do not have to conform.

—Marva Nettles Collins

Toi Derricotte, poet. Photo by by Nat Clymer.

"The fact that white people readily and proudly call themselves "white," glorify all that is white, and whitewash all that is glorified, becomes unnatural and bigoted in its intent only when these same whites deny persons of African heritage who are black the natural and inalienable right to readily—proudly—call themselves "black," glorify all that is black, and blackwash all that is glorified."

—Abbey Lincoln (b. 1930)
"Who Will Revere the Black Woman?" *Negro Digest*,
September 1966

AUGUST

6 In 1969, **Milicent V. Boney** became the first Black woman in the United States to own and operate an investment company.

During the 1948 summer Olympic Games in London, **Alice Coachman** became the first Black woman to win a gold medal in the high jump. **7**

8 In 1862, **Mary Jane Patterson** became the first Black woman to receive a Bachelor of Arts degree when she graduated from Oberlin College in Ohio.

Pop vocalist, actress **Whitney Houston** was born on this day in 1963. **9**

AUGUST

10 The doyenne of "Black Society" journalism in her day, **Gerri (Geraldyn) Hodges Major** was born in 1894.

Catherine Ferguson established the first Sunday school in New York City in the 1790s. **11**

12 **Gladys Bentley**, a Black lesbian entertainer in the 1920s and the 1930s, was born on this day in 1907.

1987 and 1988 Grammy Award winner, operatic soprano **Kathleen Battle** was born on this day in 1948. **13**

You never git nothing by bein' an angel child.
You better change yo ways and git real wild.
I'm gonna tell you something, wouldn't tell you no lie.
Wild women are the only kind that every git by.
Wild women don't worry, they don't have no blues.

—Ida Cox, blueswoman, from
"Wild Women Don't Have the Blues"

Not to know is bad; not to wish to know is worse.

—Nigerian proverb

Photo courtesy of Smithsonian Institution

"The difference between white and black females seemed to me an eminently satisfactory one. White females were ladies, said the sign maker, worthy of respect. And the quality that made ladyhood worthy? Softness, helplessness, and modesty—which I interpreted as a willingness to let others do their labor and their thinking. Colored females, on the other hand, were women unworthy of respect—independent and immodest."

—Toni Morrison (b. 1931)
"What the Black Woman Thinks about Women's Lib,"
New York Times Magazine, August 22, 1971

AUGUST

14 The first Black woman war correspondent was **Ethel Payne**, who reported from Vietnam. She was born on this day in 1911. From 1953 to 1973 she was the one-person White House correspondent for the *Chicago Defender*. She's known as "the First Lady of the Black Press."

15 In 1990, **Maxine Waters** became the second Black woman from California to be elected to the U.S. Congress. She was born on this day in 1938.

16 **Queen Ranavalona I** of Madagascar reigned from 1828 until her death on this day in 1861.

17 **Maria Stewart** was the first Black woman born in the United States to lecture in public. She made her first speech in Boston in 1832.

AUGUST

18 In 1859, **Harriet E. Wilson** became the first Black to publish a novel in the United States with the publication of her novel *Our Nig: Or Sketches From the Life of a Free Black in a Two-Story White House Showing That Slavery's Shadows Fall Even There.*

Lena Wright Myers became the first Black woman to earn a Ph.D., in sociology and social psychology, from Michigan State University in 1973. **19**

20 In 1619, **Isabella**, the first Black woman to the New World on record, arrived in Jamestown, Virginia, on a Dutch man-of-war with a boatload of other Africans captured from a Spanish frigate bound for the West Indies.

Harriet M. West became the first Black woman to attain the rank of major in 1943 in the Women's Army Auxiliary Corps (WAACs). **21**

AUGUST

22 In 1974, **Hazel Garland** became the first Black woman to work as editor-in-chief of the nationally circulated *Pittsburgh Courier*.

Elizabeth Williams, born on this day in 1923, was the first Black WAAC to attend and graduate from the Fort Monmouth Photo Division School, New Jersey. She achieved a superior rating and established a new high record of scholastic achievement. Later, she became an intelligence photographer for the Army. **23**

What I really believe is that we as a people must be consciously aware that we must perpetuate ourselves and some idea of ourselves.

—Shirley Anne Williams

Family photo from the collection of Stephanie Byrd

"My great-grandmama told my grandmama the part she lived through that my grandmama didn't live through and my grandmama told my mama what they both lived through and my mama told me what they all lived through and we were suppose to pass it down like that from generation to generation so we'd never forget."

—Gayl Jones (b. 1949)
Corregidora (1975)

AUGUST

24 **Lorna Simpson**, the first Black woman to have a solo exhibition of painting and sculpture at the Museum of Modern Art in New York City, was born in 1960.

Choreographer **Debbie Allen** and actresses **Lynn Whitfield**, **Ruby Dee**, and **Madge Sinclair** won Emmys in 1991. **25**

26 In 1937, **Rose Butler Brown** became the first Black woman to receive a Ph.D. from Harvard's Graduate School of Education.

Phyllis Garland earned a journalism degree at Northwestern University in 1957 and was the only Black in the graduating class. She began her career at *Ebony* and went on to teach at Columbia University Graduate School of Journalism. She is the daughter of Hazel Garland. *(See August 22.)* **27**

AUGUST

28 On this day in 1988, actress **Beah Richards** won an Emmy for her role in the television series "Frank's Place."

29 Rhythm and blues and jazz vocalist **Dinah Washington** was born on this day in 1924.

Wyomia Tyus, the first man or woman to win Olympic gold medals for the same event in consecutive Olympic Games (Tokyo '64/Mexico City '68), was born on this day in 1945.

30 The first Black woman to host a television show in the South, Xernona Clayton (Brady), worked for WAGA-TV in Atlanta, Georgia, in the 1960s. She was born on this day in 1930.

31 Nationally renowned and revolutionary educator **Marva Collins** founded Westside Preparatory School in Chicago in 1975. The school is an alternative, progressive educational institution for Black children on Chicago's neglected and maligned West Side. Marva Collins was born on this day in 1936.

Having overcome as a race and a sex so many obstacles that to the fainting, faltering heart seemed insurmountable in the past, we shall neither be discouraged at the temporary failures of our friends, not frightened at the apparent success of our foes.

—Mary Church Terrell

I often say to people that I have a right to shout more than some folks; I have been bought twice, and set free twice, and so I feel I have a good right to shout. Hallelujah!

—Amanda Berry Smith, itinerant preacher, born in Maryland in 1837

Photo from Stephanie Byrd's collection

"Racial oppression of black people in America has done what neither class oppression nor sexual oppression, with all their perniciousness, has ever done: destroyed an entire people and their culture."

—Eleanor Holmes Norton (b. 1937)
"For Sadie and Maude," *Sisterhood is Powerful,*
Robin Morgan, ed. (1970)

SEPTEMBER

1 Writer **Rosa Guy** was born on this day in 1925.

2 The **Female Literary Association of Philadelphia** (Black women only) held its first meeting in 1834. Women in the group submitted unsigned works to be critiqued by each other. Their works were often published in the abolitionist paper *The Liberator*.

3 **Eva Jessye**, world renowned choral conductor and arranger, composed "When the Saints Go Marching In" as well as other spirituals. She was born in 1895.

4 The National Guard stopped fifteen-year-old **Elizabeth Eckford** at the door when she arrived at school by herself and attempted to enter Central High School in Little Rock, Arkansas, on this day in 1957.

SEPTEMBER

5 In 1820, **Maria Becraft**, at age 15, opened the first boarding school for Black girls in Washington, D.C.

Mattiwilda Dobbs, the first Black member of the Metropolitan Opera Company, made her debut as Gilda in *Rigoletto* in 1956. **6**

7 Longtime curator— from 1955 to her retirement in 1984— and chief of the **Schomberg Center for Research in Black Culture** in New York City, **Jean Blackwell Hutson** oversaw the largest collection on Black culture and literature. She was born on this day in 1914.

Saundra Williams was crowned the first Miss Black America on this day in 1968. **8**

Marjorie Judith Vincent of Illinois was selected as the fourth Black Miss America in 1990.

SEPTEMBER

9 Poet, writer, and playwright **Sonia Sanchez** was born on this day in 1934.

10 One of the first modern Black female poets of the twentieth century, **Georgia Douglas Johnson** was born on this day in 1880.

Community empowerment means the strengthening of those who head households. In the inner city, that means organizing and empowering Black women.

—Patrice Johnson, editor of *The Black Commentator*

"Ours was a marriage, a love affair—the land would nurture us, and we would honor the land. But the land was too rich and too good. The powerful and greedy invaders saw this at once....We Africans were not consulted or even paid attention to. We were pushed aside, robbed of our land. When we protested, we were massacred. A handful of whites took power, and with their boots they pressed the faces of an entire people to the dirt."

—Miriam Makeba (b. 1932)
prologue, *Makeba, My Story,* with James Hall (1987)

SEPTEMBER

11 "The First Lady of Las Vegas," dancer and performer **Lola Folana** was born on this day in 1943.

12 The first **Black branch** of the Young Women's Christian Association (YWCA) was opened in Dayton, Ohio, in 1893.

13 **Isabel Sanford** won an Emmy for her role in the TV comedy series "The Jeffersons" on this day in 1981.

14 In October 1995, **Mrs. Margaret Rose Campbelle** died at age 109. A retired teacher in the Florida public school system, she was welcomed back to the 1994 commencement ceremonies at Clark Atlanta University, her alma mater, as the institution's oldest living graduate.

SEPTEMBER

15 **Addie Collins, Denise McNair, Carol Robertson,** and **Cynthia Wesley** were killed in the bombing of the 16th Street Baptist Church in Birmingham, Alabama, on this day in 1963. This violent act galvanized the Civil Rights Movement.

Ntozake Shange's *for colored girls who have considered suicide when the rainbow is enuf* opened this month on Broadway at the Booth Theatre in 1976. *(See also October 18.)* **16**

17 **Vanessa Williams** was crowned the first Black Miss America on this day in 1983. *(See also July 23.)*

Mary Morris Burnett Talbert was born this day in 1866. *(See also November 21.)*

In 1939, when **Elise Ayers** was appointed as a principal in the New York City public school system, she became the first Black woman in the twentieth century to hold that position in the United States. **18**

I have wrapped myself in my people's essence,
learned to wear Africa's stole
of dark, soft energy like night vapors
rising from rainsoaked furrows;...

—Aneb Kgositsile from "Fourth Decade"

Hit one ring and the whole chain will
resound.

—Sotho proverb

We need to dig and jump into the land we
come from; one woman after another, one
dream upon the other, calling up who we are.

—Ntozake Shange

Photo by James Van Der Zee "Tap Dancer NYC," 1935

"Sarah: I wanted to live in Genesis in the midst of golden savannas, nim and white frankopenny trees and white stallions roaming under a blue sky. I wanted to walk with a white dove."

—Marita Bonner (b. 1899)
Funnyhouse of a Negro (1964)

SEPTEMBER

19 On this day in 1968, when NBC-TV premiered "Julia" starring **Diahann Carroll**, this series became the first to star a Black woman since "Beulah" ran in the 1950s.

20 Actress **Alfre Woodard** won an Emmy for best supporting actress for a role on the television series "L.A. Law" in 1984. She was also an Academy Award nominee for best supporting actress.

21 Actress **Diana Sands** died of cancer on this day in 1973. Contemporary, un-typed, and intelligent, she offered an entirely new theater persona for Black women. She performed on Broadway, in Shakespeare, and in Hollywood movies.

22 **Mollie Moon** (1912–1990) was an organizer and the first president of the National Urban League Guild, a fund-raising organization for the Urban League.

SEPTEMBER

23 **Miriam Tlati** was the first Black woman to publish a novel in South Africa.

24 In 1978, **Cardiss Collins** became the first woman to chair the congressional Black Caucus. She was born on this day in 1931.

25 In 1928, **Daisy Lampkin** (1883–1965) was the first Black woman elected as a delegate-at-large from Pennsylvania to the Republican National Convention.

26 The first Black woman bank president in the United States, **Maggie L. Walker**, was born on this day in 1867. The bank she managed, the Saint Luke Penny Savings Bank, opened in 1903.

SEPTEMBER

27 **Natalie Hinderas** was one of the first Black concert pianists to be managed by a major studio (Columbia) in the 1950s.

In 1986, **Niara Sudarkasa** became **28** the first Black woman president of Lincoln University in Pennsylvania.

If we are not afraid to adopt a revolutionary stance—if, indeed, we wish to be radical in our quest for change—then we must get to the root of our oppression. After all, radical simply means "grasping things at the root."

—Angela Y. Davis

JOSEPHINE BAKER
(1906–1975)

Born into extreme poverty in St. Louis, Baker survived and became a dresser for a theater company in the city of her birth. Baker finally made her way to Rochester, New York in 1924, where she got a part as a chorus girl in Bainville. From there she moved to (New York City) where she appeared at the Plantation Club. She was approached by Caroline Dudley to join a troupe of Black actors who would be working in Paris; when asked by Dudley if she could sing and dance, Baker said yes, even though she couldn't keep a beat. She revealed her unschooled talent on board the ship to Paris. Again Baker turned a bad situation into one that would propel her to stardom. Baker spent the rest of her life in France, except for brief visits to America. She was awarded the Legion of Honor for her work with the French underground during World War II. The adoptive mother of twelve children, Baker was an early believer in multiculturalism as a solution to racism and bigotry in the world.

—from *Josephine*, by Josephine Baker and Jo Bouillon, translated from the French by Mariana Fitzpatrick (Harper & Row, 1977)

SEPTEMBER/OCTOBER

29 **Agnes Wheaton**, born in 1907, was the first Black woman to coach and manage the oldest track team in Massachusetts, the Red Diamond Athletic Club.

In 1952, *Gold Through the Trees* **30** became the first play written by a Black woman, **Alice Childress**, to be professionally produced on stage in the United States. *(See also October 12.)*

1 In 1930, Paramount's "race" series made its first release, "Daddy Blues" and "Don't Pan Me," recorded by **Alberta Hunter** (born in 1895).

In 1885, **Sarah E. Good** patented a folding cabinet. **2**

OCTOBER

3   **"Beulah"** premiered on ABC-TV on this day in 1950. The show starred Ethel Waters, who took over the role originated by Hattie McDaniel on the radio show of the same name. *(See also June 14.)*

Bernice J. Reagon, an original member of the SNCC Freedom Singers and founder of the a cappella female vocal ensemble **Sweet Honey In the Rock**, was born on this day in 1942.   **4**

5   During this month in 1995, **Sandra Trim-DaCosta**, director of marketing of GRP Records in New York, was named vice-president of marketing for the company. She now supervises all marketing activities for the Impulse!, GRP, and Blue Thumb labels.

Activist **Fannie Lou Hamer** was born on this day in 1917. *(See also March 15.)*   **6**

We are positively a unique people.
Breathtaking people.
Anything we do, we do big! Despite
attempts to stereotype us,
we are crazy, individual and
uncorral-able people.

> —Leontyne Price, b. 1927 in Laurel,
> Mississippi, "Prima Donna Absoluta"

Mundu muka na iguru itimenyagirwo.
Woman and sky cannot be understood.
(Woman, wind and fortune are ever
changing.)

> —Kikuyu proverb

...it is the women of a country who
help to mold its character, and to influ-
ence if not determine its destiny....

> —Frances E. W. Harper, 19th century

Maya Angelou
(b. 1928)

Born in St. Louis, Missouri, Maya Angelou née Marguerite Johnson is a poet, dancer, journalist, and lecturer. Her most popularly read autobiography, *I Know Why the Caged Bird Sings*, has been adapted and performed throughout the world and serves as an inspiration to young Black women worldwide. A generous and expansive instructor, Angelou has not only given of her expertise to her students but also opened her heart to those who are seeking a message of hope. She presently teaches master writing classes at the University of North Carolina-Chapel Hill.

OCTOBER

7 **Mother Charleszetta Waddles**, a one-woman war on poverty and ordained minister in Detroit, Michigan, was born on this day in 1912. She founded and acted as director of the Perpetual Mission for Saving Souls of All Nations.

Visual artist **Faith Ringgold** was born on this day in 1930. **8**

9 In Windsor, Canada, in the mid-1800s, **Mary Ann Camberton Shadd (Cary)** was the first Black woman in North America to establish a weekly newspaper. She was born on this day in 1823.

During late 1995, Police Chief **Beverly Harvard** became the nation's first Black woman to head a major city police department in Atlanta, Georgia. **10**

OCTOBER

11 The "Black Nun of Moret," **Louise-Marie**, the illegitimate daughter of Queen Marie-Theresa, wife of King Louis XIV of France, died in a convent in 1732.

12 **Cheryl Glass**, the first Black driver in the Indianapolis 500, was born on this day in 1961.

Alice Childress was born this day in 1920. In 1955, her play Trouble in Mind was the first play by a Black woman to win an Obie Award. *(See also September 30.)*

13 **Edith Sampson**, the first Black woman U.S. delegate to the United Nations, was born on this day in 1901.

14 In 1920, the first blues singer on record, **Mamie Smith**, sold 75,000 copies in one month of her first recording, "Crazy Blues."

OCTOBER

15 Zina Garrison was the first Black woman to rank in the top ten tennis players since the women's professional tennis tournament began in 1971. She beat Martina Navratilova (ranked number one) in 1986 in the quarterfinals in the United States Open.

In 1995, **Deirdre Hughes Hill** was elected president of the Los Angeles Police Commission. She is both the youngest and the first Black woman ever elected to this position. **16**

The essence of a free life is being able to choose the style of living you prefer free from exclusion and without the compulsion of conformity or law.

—Eleanor Holmes Norton, equal rights activist, born 1937. Commencement Address, Barnard College, NY, June 6, 1972

NTOZAKE SHANGE
(B. 1948)

Born in Trenton, New Jersey, Shange moved to St. Louis, Missouri, at the age of eight and had her first experience of racial segregation. She graduated from Barnard College in 1970 and in 1973 earned her masters in American Studies from the University of Southern California. Shange utilizes a mixture of poetry, music, and dance to create drama that celebrates African American women and their ability to survive physical and emotional abuse. She gained national and international attention with her 1975 play *for colored girls who have considered suicide when the rainbow is enuf.* Shange, who attempted suicide many times, has managed to convert her demons into art.

OCTOBER

17 The first and thus far the only Black woman astronaut, **Mae C. Jennison**, was born on this day in 1956.

18 Writer, dancer, and choreoplaywright **Ntozake Shange** was born Paulette Williams on this day in 1948. *(See also September 16.)*

19 In late 1995, **Kathy Waters** was named manager of Maryland's MARC Commuter Rail System Administration's Office of Transit Operation. She is the first Black woman in Maryland to manage a commuter rail service.

20 Food chemist **Cecile Hoover Edwards** was born in 1926. Her research has advanced the understanding of the composition of food, radioisotopes, and microbiological assays of amino acids and vitamins.

OCTOBER

21 In 1971, **Francis Cole**, the first known Black harpsichord player, received a standing ovation at Carnegie Recital Hall in New York City.

Christia Daniels Adair, suffragette, civil rights leader, and politician for more than 40 years in Texas, was born on this day in 1893. **22**

23 In the late 1930s, **Thelma Gorham** (born in 1913) became the only woman editor for the *Apache Sentinel*, an official U.S. Army publication at Fort Huachuca, Arizona.

In 1856, **Charlotte Forten Grimke** became the first Black to teach white students in Massachusetts. **24**

It is a real fact that wherever you want anything done, teach a woman how to do it and in a few days you will have the same thing in various beautiful uncountable numbers.

—Councillor Rushwaya for Shurugwi,
Zimbabwe, 1983

If I actually ran the world, I'd do it from the kitchen. It's not anything deliberate or a statement or anything, that's just how I understand things. It's arranged along informal lines.

—Jamaica Kincaid

...if we focus exclusively on sexism and racism we remain mired in the myths we are trying to dissipate.

—Elizabeth Fox-Genovese

LORRAINE HANSBERRY
(1930–1965)

Born in Chicago, Hansberry
studied painting at the Art
Institute of Chicago and later
attended the University of
Wisconsin and the New
School for Social Research in
New York. When she moved
to New York in the 1950s she
also began writing plays and
short stories. She supported
herself by working an assort-
ment of jobs until completing
A Raisin in the Sun in 1957.
She received the New York
Drama Critics Circle Award
for Best American Play of
1958–1959. *A Raisin in the Sun*
was the first Broadway play
written by a Black woman and
the first Broadway play to be
directed by a Black director in
51 years. After her death, her
notes and parts of her published work were adapted for a
theater production called *To
Be Young Gifted and Black*. It
opened on Broadway in
November 1969.

OCTOBER

25 **Marita Bonner** was awarded an Obie Award in 1964 for the off-Broadway production of her play, *Funnyhouse of a Negro.*

In 1869, **Lillie G. Taylor** became one of the richest Black women in the world when the Massachusetts Supreme Court ruled that a vast amount of oil- and gas-rich land in Louisiana belonged to her. **26**

27 Actress **Ruby Dee** was born Ruby Ann Wallace on this day in 1927.

In 1969, **Victoria Lynn Sanders** became Chicago's first Black stockbroker. **28**

OCTOBER/NOVEMBER

29 **Harriet Powers**, the creator of the renowned "Bible Quilts" at the National Museum of History and Technology in the Smithsonian Institution in Washington, D.C., was born on this day in 1837.

Dr. Matilda Arabella Evans (1870s–1935) organized, established, and practiced medicine at Columbia, South Carolina's first hospital for black patients. She was the first woman licensed to practice medicine in South Carolina. **30**

31 The first woman to perform W. C. Handy's "St. Louis Blues," blues singer and actress **Ethel Waters** was born on this day in 1900. *(See also June 14.)*

Singer, dancer, and comedienne **Florence Mills**, or "Little Twink," died at age 32 on this day in 1927. She achieved stage success in *Shuffle Along* in 1922. **1**

NOVEMBER

2 **Katie B. Hall**
was elected and
became the first
Black congressional repre-
sentative from Indiana on
this day in 1982.

Carrie Saxon Perry **3**
was elected and
became the first Black
woman mayor of a
Connecticut city, Hartford
(defeating a white male
Republican 10,304 votes to
7,613), in 1987.

Learn to be quiet enough to hear the
sound of the genuine within yourself so
that you can hear it in other people.

—Marian Wright Edelman

JUNE JORDAN
(B. 1936)

Educated at Barnard College
and the University of Chicago,
Jordan was the winner of the
Rockefeller Fellowship in
Creative Writing, 1969–1970,
and the Rome Prize Fellowship in Environmental Design,
1970–1971. A poet, dramatist,
educator, and activist, Jordan
contributes to such journals as
The Progressive and is the
author of *I Was Looking at the
Ceiling and then I Saw the Sky*.
She was born in Harlem and
later taught English at CCNY
and Connecticut College. She
now lives in California.

Photo by Sara Miles

NOVEMBER

4 In 1946, **Alice Dunnigan** became the first Black woman accredited to the White House press corps. She was the first female sportswriter in Washington, D.C., and the first Black correspondent to travel with a president (Harry Truman during his 1948 campaign).

5 In 1937, **Jackie Ormes**, the creator of "Torchy Brown in Dixie to Harlem," became the first Black woman cartoonist to create a nationally syndicated comic strip.

6 **Sharon Pratt Kelly** became the first woman to win the mayoral race in Washington, D.C., on this day in 1990.

7 The first Black woman neurosurgeon in the United States, **Alexa Canady**, was born on this day in 1950. She was certified by the American Board of Neurological Surgery in 1984.

NOVEMBER

8 Sculptor **Meta Vaux Warrick Fuller** died on this day in 1968. She was one of the United States' first prominent Black sculptors. *(See also Janunary 22.)*

Dorothy Dandridge was the first Black woman to be nominated for an Oscar (for her role in *Carmen Jones*). She was born on this day in 1923. **9**

10 **Ida Cox**, the composer of the blues classic "Wild Women Don't Get the Blues," died on this day in 1968.

The **Bethune Museum and Archives**, a depository and center for Black women's history, was established in Washington, D.C., on this day in 1979. **11**

You know, it would probably be easier for me not to speak out, not to ever say anything about the issues of sexual harassment or the role of women in the workplace and politics, not talk about those things ever again in life. But I think it would be irresponsible for me not to say what I really believe in my heart to be true—that there are some serious inequities we face as women and that we can work to address these inequities. I will not be satisfied anymore with living my life simply for myself. Other issues are much broader than my own little world.

—Anita Hill

ALICE WALKER
(B. 1944)

Born in Eatonton, Georgia, Walker was the eighth child born to her sharecropper parents. Due to a childhood injury to her eyesight, she became introspective and observant. She marks that incident as the emergence of her "inner vision." Walker attended Spelman College and received her B.A. from Sarah Lawrence in 1965. She taught Black Studies at Jackson State College and Tougaloo College, as well as lecturing at Wellesley and the University of Massachusetts. She has been a fellow at the Radcliffe Institute and received a National Endowment of the Arts Grant in 1969. In 1982, she won the Pulitzer Prize and the American Book Award for her novel *The Color Purple*. She resides in California and is the mother of a daughter.

Photo by Nan E. Park

NOVEMBER

12 The **Sigma Gamma Rho** sorority was founded on this day in 1922 in Indianapolis. With "Greater Service, Greater Progress" as its motto, it was the first Black sorority on a predominantly white campus, Butler University.

13 Actress and comedienne **Whoopi Goldberg** was born Caryn Johnson on this day in 1949. *(See also March 9.)*

14 In 1984, **Kristina Smith** (born in 1964) became the first Black Tournament of Roses queen in the pageant's 67-year history.

15 With the production of *The Girl at the Fort*, the **Anita Bush Stock Theatre Company** made its debut at the New Lincoln Theatre in Harlem on this day in 1915. This Black dramatic stock company performed serious, nonmusical theater for Black audiences and grew to be a training ground for hundreds of Black actors.

NOVEMBER

16 In 1970, when **Dr. Frances Cress Welsing**, noted psychiatrist and author, introduced the Cress theory of color confrontation and racism, she was denied tenure at the Howard University Medical School. However, she continued as staff psychiatrist (1967–1991) at the District of Columbia's Department of Human Services. From 1976 to 1990, she was also the clinical director of the Paul Robeson School for Growth and Development. She continues now in private practice.

The first Black poet laureate of New York State (1991), **Audre Lorde**, died on this day in 1992. **17**

18 In 1977, a Ku Klux Klan member was convicted of first-degree murder in connection with the church bombing that killed four young Black girls in Birmingham, Alabama, in 1963. *(See also September 15.)*

In 1983, **Dianne Dunham** became the first Black female to win the U.S. Gymnastics Championship. **19**

NOVEMBER

20 In 1968, representing the Bedford Stuyvesant section of Brooklyn, New York, **Shirley Chisolm** became the first Black woman elected to Congress. Four years later, in 1972, she campaigned for president of the United States. She was born on this day in 1924.

In 1922, **Mary Morris Burnett Talbert** was the first Black woman to receive the NAACP Springarn Medal. She was also appointed assistant principal of Bethel University—the only woman ever selected for that position. In 1887, she became the principal of Union High School in Little Rock, Arkansas. She was an elected president of the National Association of Colored Women (NACW) and served for two terms as vice-president of the NAACP. She was a board member of the NAACP until her death in 1923. *(See also September 17.)* **21**

T hose who consider themselves to be revolutionary must begin to deal with other revolutionaries as equals. And so far as I know, revolutionaries are not determined by sex.

—Frances Beal

SHIRLEY CHISHOLM
(B. 1924)

Chisholm began her career as a teacher and director of New York City nursery schools and was later recognized as an authority on early education and child welfare. In 1964 she became a member of the New York State Assembly. In 1969 she was the first Black woman ever elected to the House of Representatives. She also co-chaired the National Political Congress of Black Women. In 1972, as a presidential candidate, Chisholm won ten percent of the democratic convention vote. She has also received honorary doctorates from 31 institutions and has been inducted into the National Women's Hall of Fame. Her success gives hope to women and other minorities considering a run for office. Chisholm stressed the need for a multicultural education in America due to stereotypical thinking about many groups. Her way of advancing multicultural thinking has been to actively fight for fair laws and equality among all groups.

NOVEMBER

22 The "Black Marilyn Monroe" of the early 1950s, **Joyce Bryant**, had a trademark for wearing skintight, backless, fishtail dresses.

Imitation of Life, starring **Louise Beavers** and **Fredi Washington**, premiered in New York City on this day in 1934. **23**

24 Ex-slave **Elizabeth Forth Denison** (1752–1866) gave the idea and $1,000 of her life's savings to help build the First St. James Episcopal Church in Grosse Ile, Michigan. It was completed in 1867.

Tina Turner was born Annie Mae Bullock on this day in 1941. **25**

NOVEMBER

26 **Sojourner Truth** died on this day in 1883. Her gravesite is in Battle Creek, Michigan. *(See also June 1.)*

In 1989, **Jennifer Lawson** not only became the first woman chief programming executive for PBS-TV, but she also became the first Black woman to hold this position at any major TV network. **27**

28 In 1981, **Pam McAllister Johnson** became the first Black woman to head a general circulation newspaper— Gannett's *Ithaca Journal* (in New York State)—in the United States.

In 1937, the all-girl's band, the **International Sweethearts of Rhythm**, was organized at the Piney Woods School for the poor and orphaned in Mississippi. **29**

... I particularly appeal to readers who are female and black, to continue the examination of your life experiences, to identify the threads of style, authenticity, strength and sensitivity running through them, to value them and share them (whether wanted or not by those around you) in whatever form is yours, in stories, in performing, in formal speeches, or in research.

—Dr. Carole A. Oglesby

I don't drink or do any drugs. I never have and I never will. I don't need them. I'm a Black woman from the land of the free, home of the brave and I figure I don't need another illusion.

—Bertice Berry

MA RAINEY
(1886–1939)

Born in Columbus, Georgia
and originally named Gertrude
Malissa Nix Pridgett, Rainey
made her first public appear-
ance at the age of twelve as
part of a show at a local opera
house. In 1904 she married
William 'Pa' Rainey. Around
this time she began singing in
Cabarets and toured with the
Rabbit Foot Minstrels and Tol-
liver's Circus. After many years
of being on the road, in 1923
Paramount began recording
her simple, direct blues style on
a series of records that brought
her belated fame. In the early
1930s Bessie Smith, who had
been a former protegé, shared
the bill with her at the Fort
Worth Stock Show. In 1933
upon the death of her mother,
Rainey retired from music and
settled in Rome, Georgia where
she remained till her death.

NOVEMBER/DECEMBER

30 **Judith Jamison** debuted with the Alvin Ailey American Dance Theater in Chicago on this day in 1965. She brought her statuesque height (six feet) and natural hair style to redefine the image of women in dance. She broke the barriers of the dance world and inspired an entire generation of aspiring dancers. She was named artistic director in 1990, becoming the first Black woman to direct a major modern dance company.

1 In 1995, **Jennifaye V. Brown**, a physical therapist at Dekalb Medical Center in Decatur, Georgia, became the first Black Georgia clinical specialist in neurology certified by the American Board of Physical Therapy Specialties.

2 In 1942, the first two companies (three hundred women) of Black WAACs completed basic training and were sent to Fort Huachuca, Arizona.

3 In 1964, **Donale Luna** from Detroit, Michigan, became the first Black female model to appear on the cover of a fashion magazine. She also became first to earn top fees.

DECEMBER

4 The first book of poetry by a Black person in the colonies was published in 1773 and written by **Phillis Wheatley,** who was born in Senegal, West Africa, and sold as a slave in 1761.

5 In 1993, actress **Mary Alice** won an Emmy for Best Supporting Actress for her role in the television drama "I'll Fly Away."

6 **Alpha Kappa Alpha**, founded in 1908 at Howard University, was the first Greek-letter organization for Black women in the United States.

7 Journalist **Carole Simpson** was born on this day in 1940. In 1988, she began anchoring "World News Saturday" for the ABC television network.

DECEMBER

8 In 1985, **Dr. Edith Irby Jones** (born in 1927) was elected the first woman president of the National Medical Association.

9 Elected a Fellow of London's Royal Society of Arts, painter **Lois Mailou Jones** is in 16 permanent collections in the United States and abroad.

We must concentrate on what we can do and erase "can't," "won't" and "don't think so" from our vocabulary.

—Cardiss Collins

ROSA PARKS
(B. 1913)

Parks was born Rosa McCauley in Tuskegee, Alabama. Wanting her daughter to be well educated, Parks' mother saved money to be able to send her to a private school for Black girls in Montgomery. At nineteen she married Raymond Parks and three years later she finished high school. Despite her education, Parks was unable to find work, and was reduced to being a seamstress. Her growing frustration with segregation caused her to join the NAACP. There, her intelligence was recognized and she was asked to become the secretary for the Alabama branch. As she became more of an activist, some friends urged her to take a workshop at Highlander Folk School, a progressive anti-segregation organization. It was in that same year that Rosa refused to give up her bus seat to a white man, which started the famous Montgomery bus boycott. In her later years Parks was elected to the board of directors of the NAACP and founded the Raymond and Rosa Parks Institute of Self-Development.

DECEMBER

10 In 1944, **Doris E. Spears** became the first woman deputy sheriff in Los Angeles, California.

Willie Mae "Big Mama" Thornton, **11** who recorded the song "Hound Dog" (which Elvis Presley later made famous), was born on this day in 1926.

12 Vocalist **Dionne Warwick** was born on this day in 1941.

Ella Baker was born on this day in 1903. **13** She played a key role in the formation of the Student Nonviolent Coordinating Committee (SNCC) and the Mississippi Freedom Democratic Party in the 1960s.

DECEMBER

14 Author **Nella Larson** was the first Black woman to receive a Guggenheim Award.

15 The great-grandmother of W. E. B. DuBois, **Elizabeth "Mumbet" Freeman**, died on this date in 1829. She successfully petitioned for her freedom from slavery in Massachusetts in 1781.

16 **Augusta Savage** was one of four women and the only Black woman commissioned in 1937 to produce a piece of sculpture for the New York World's Fair of 1939–1940.

17 **Queen Nzingha**, who fought the Portuguese conquest of Angola, died on this day in 1663.

DECEMBER

18 **Mary Schmidt Campbell** (born in 1948) was the former executive director of the **Studio Museum** in Harlem, the first Black museum to be accredited.

Actress **Cicely Tyson** was born on this day in 1933. **19**

20 **Jennifer Holliday** won a Tony Award for her role in *DreamGirls*, which premiered on Broadway at the Imperial Theatre on this day in 1981.

Born on this day in 1959, runner **Florence Griffith "Flo Jo" Joyner** won three gold medals and a silver medal in the 1988 Olympics in Seoul, Korea. She set a new World Record in the 200 meter event. **21**

ELENA FEATHERSTON
(B. 1947)

Featherston works as a writer, lecturer, workshop leader, and is the producer/director of the award-winning documentary *Alice Walker: Visions of the Spirit*. She is the founder of Featherston and Associates, a group of cross-cultural trainers specializing in gender and racial equity issues. A political visionary who concentrates in social theory and human development, she has lectured throughout the United States and Europe since 1982. She is a counselor and group leader for a variety of cross-cultural concerns. A long-time activist, Featherston is involved in many political movements including Civil and Human Rights, the Women's Movement, the Anti-Nuclear Movement, and movements for Freedom, Peace and Justice in South Africa. She is the editor of the book *Skin Deep; Women Writing on Color, Culture, and Identity,* The Crossing Press, 1994. Her recent film and video project is *Under Our Skins: Interracial Relationships*, an exploration of cross-cultural relationships from the perspectives of women of color.

Photo by Lorene Warwick

DECEMBER

22 With her doctorate of economics in 1921, **Sadie Alexander** became the first Black woman in the nation to earn a doctorate degree. Six years later, in 1927, she became the first Black woman to graduate from the University of Pennsylvania Law School.

In 1919, **Alice H. Parker** received a patent for a gas-heating furnace. **23**

24 "Mother of the Blues," **"Ma Rainey,"** was the first blues singer who entertained from the turn of the twentieth century to the Depression. She was born Gertrude Pridgett in 1886.

By dressing as a slavemaster and with her husband as a slave, **Ellen Craft** escaped bondage when she arrived in Philadelphia from Macon, Georgia, in 1848. **25**

DECEMBER

26 Today is the first day of Kwanzaa: *umoja* ("unity").

Today is the second day of Kwanzaa: *kujichagulia* ("self-determination"). **27**

In 1937, **La Julia Rhea** sang in the Chicago City Opera Company's production of Verdi's *Aida* and thus was the first to integrate the nation's opera.

28 Today is the third day of Kwanzaa: *ujima* ("collective work and responsibility").

In 1977, **Karen Farmer** became the first Black member of the Daughters of the American Revolution.

Today is the fourth day of Kwanzaa: *ujamaa* ("cooperative economics"). **29**

Ethelene Crockett, the first Black woman obstetrician-gynecologist in Michigan, died on this day in 1978.

DECEMBER

30 Today is the fifth day of Kwanzaa: *nia* ("purpose").

Today is the sixth day of Kwanzaa: *kuumba* ("creativity"). **31**

Odetta, the internationally renowned folksinger, was born on this day in 1930.

Everybody has their place of just absolute brilliance and I *want* that. I want everybody to be in that place of self-knowledge and ecstasy, cause that means we're all free.

—Rachel Bagby

To receive a current catalog from
The Crossing Press
please call toll-free,
800-777-1048.